DIGGING FOR TRICERATOPS

BY THOMAS R. HOLTZ JR., Ph.D.

A Discovery

TIMELINE

CAPSTONE PRESS
a capstone imprint

Capstone Press
1710 Roe Crest Drive
North Mankato, Minnesota 56003
www.capstonepub.com

Our very special thanks to Mike Brett-Surman, PhD, Museum Specialist for
Fossil Dinosaurs, Reptiles, Amphibians, and Fish at the National Museum of
Natural History, Smithsonian Institution, for his curatorial review. Capstone would
also like to thank Kealy Wilson, Product Development Manager, and the following
at Smithsonian Enterprises: Ellen Nanney, Licensing Manager; Brigid Ferraro,
Vice President, Education and Consumer Products; Carol LeBlanc,
Senior Vice President, Education and Consumer Products.

Library of Congress Cataloging-in-Publication Data
Holtz, Thomas R., 1965– author.
Digging for triceratops: a discovery timeline / by Thomas R. Holtz, Jr.
pages cm. — (Smithsonian. Dinosaur discovery timelines)
Summary: "Provides an annotated timeline of the discovery of Triceratops
including details on the scientists, dig sites, fossils, and other findings that have
shaped our knowledge of this dinosaur"—Provided by publisher.
Audience: Ages 8–12.
Audience: Grade 2–6.
Includes bibliographical references and index.
ISBN 978-1-4914-2126-0 (library binding)
ISBN 978-1-4914-2367-7 (paperback)
1. Triceratops—Juvenile literature. 2. Paleontology—Juvenile literature.
[1. Dinosaurs.] I. Title.
QE862.O65H664 2015
567.915'8—dc23   2014031829

Printed in Canada.
092014   008478FRS15

Editorial Credits
Kristen Mohn, editor; Lori Bye and Aruna Rangarajan, designers;
Kelly Garvin, media researcher; Kathy McColley, production specialist

Photo Credits
Alamy Images: Corbin17, 5, EPA, 22(top right), Mohamad Haghani/Stocktrek
Images, 15(top left), Nobumichi Tamura/Stocktrek Images, 25(left), Phil
Degginger, 21(tl), Sergey Krasovskiy/Stocktrek Images, 25(tr), World History
Archive, 11(tr); Corbis: AP/Michael Stravato, 26(bottom left), Bettmann, 14(tr),
16(tr); Dreamstime: Ken Backer, 19(bottom right); Getty Images: Hyoung Chang/
The Denver Post, 17(tl), Mark Hallett Paleoart, 18-19(top); Internet Archive/
Smithsonian Institution/Hatcher, J.B., O.C. Marsh & R.S. Lull, 9(right), 10(bl);
Jon Hughes, cover, backcover, 1, 10(t), 18(bl), 20(br), 23(r), 25(br), 29; Library
of Congress/Prints & Photographs Division, 7(bl); Peabody Museum of Natural
History, Yale University, 12(bl), 20(bl); Photo courtesy of Catherine Forster,
photo taken by James Clark, 21(tr); Photo courtesy of Greg Leitich Smith, 27(tr);
Photo courtesy of Xiao-chun Wu, 24(r); Science Source: 16(bl), Francois Gohier,
14(bl), 15(bl), Martin Shields, 21(bl), Roger Harris, 13, Walter Myers, 12(tr);
Shutterstock/dimair, 17(tr); University of California, Museum of Paleontology,
2014, http://ucmp.berkeley.edu, 22(bl), 23(t); Wikimedia: Agsftw, 26-27(b),
Daderot, 15(tr), Hatcher, J.B, O.C. Marsh & R.S. Lull, 6 (right), 7(tr), 8(bl); John
Ostrom/Peabody Museum, 8(bl), Momotarou2012, 17(b), O.C. Marsh, 9(tr), Lull,
11(bl), Sternberg, C.M., 7(tl)

Table of Contents

TRICERATOPS

Triceratops was one of the very last of the giant dinosaurs. No animal alive today looks anything like this three-horned beast. *Triceratops* had two huge horns above its eyes, a third horn on its nose, a frill of bone behind its head, and a body the size of a male elephant. It was a plant eater, but that doesn't mean it was harmless. After all, rhinos, bulls, and hippos are plant eaters too, and they are very dangerous.

No humans lived at the same time as *Triceratops*, so how do we know about this creature? We know about it because scientists have found and studied its fossils. Fossils are bones, teeth, footprints, and other remains that are preserved in rocks. Paleontologists—people who study fossils—use these remains to piece together the lives and habits of animals from the past.

Usually, paleontologists don't start with a complete skeleton of a dinosaur. Instead, they study the animal rock by rock, bone by bone. And this is how we learned about *Triceratops*. Here is the story of the discoveries that helped us understand the ancient three-horned dinosaur.

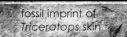

fossil imprint of
Triceratops skin

Black Butte, Wyoming; Denver and Green Mountain Creek, Colorado; Judith River and Cow Creek, Montana: *Mistaken Identities*

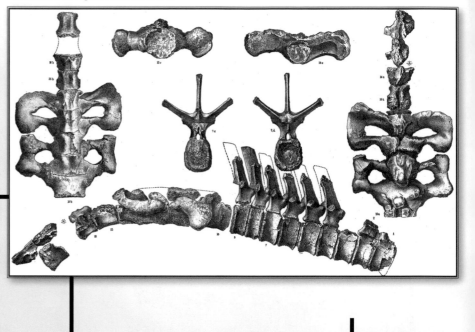

sketches of *Agathaumas* fossils

1872
Near Black Butte, geologists Fielding Bradford Meek and H. M. Bannister are working for geologist Ferdinand Hayden and paleontologist Edward Drinker Cope. They find the backbones of a giant reptile. Cope thinks this fossil is from a duckbilled dinosaur. He names it *Agathaumas* ("great wonder").

1873
Cope discovers part of a skeleton near Denver. He names it *Polyonax* ("master over many").

Monoclonius skull

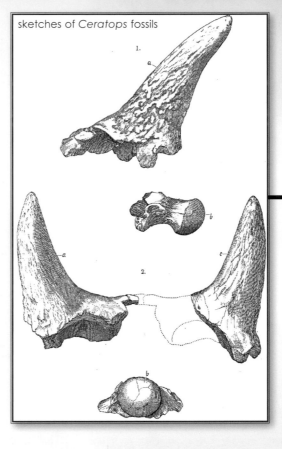
sketches of *Ceratops* fossils

1876

Near the Judith River, fossil hunter Charles H. Sternberg finds a few teeth and bones in rocks older than the ones with *Agathaumas* and *Polyonax*. He gives the fossils to Cope, who names the creature *Monoclonius* ("single stem"), based on the way the teeth fit together. At this point nobody knows that *Agathaumas*, *Polyonax*, and *Monoclonius* are horned dinosaurs.

Late Summer 1888

Fossil hunter John Bell Hatcher finds some small horns and other skull parts near Cow Creek, Montana. He sends them to Marsh, who names the creature *Ceratops* ("horned face"). The world learns that horned dinosaurs once roamed the planet.

Othniel Charles Marsh

1887

Fossil collector George Cannon finds a pair of huge horns near Green Mountain Creek. The horns are sent to paleontologist Othniel Charles Marsh of Yale University. Marsh thinks the horns come from a giant extinct bison, which he calls *Bison alticornis* ("tall horned bison").

Lusk, Wyoming: *A Three-Horned Giant*

sketch of *Stegosaurus* skeleton

Autumn 1888

Rancher Charles Guernsey shows Hatcher a horned skull sticking out of a canyon north of Lusk. Hatcher first pulls the horn out by roping it with a lasso. Then he digs out the skull, but it rolls to the bottom of the canyon. Hatcher takes the horn to Marsh, who recognizes it as the bisonlike creature. Marsh asks Hatcher to get the rest of the skull.

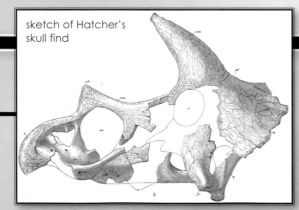

sketch of Hatcher's skull find

Marsh's fossil-hunting expedition team

August 1889

After cleaning up more of the skull, Marsh finds that there were not only two horns above the eyes, but also a third horn on the nose. He decides that this creature is different from the smaller, older *Ceratops*. He names it *Triceratops* ("three-horned face"). Marsh also names two more *Triceratops* species based on other skulls that Hatcher found. One is *Triceratops flabellatus* ("like a little fan"), after the animal's frill. The other is *Triceratops galeus* ("with a helmet").

sketches of *Triceratops'* skull

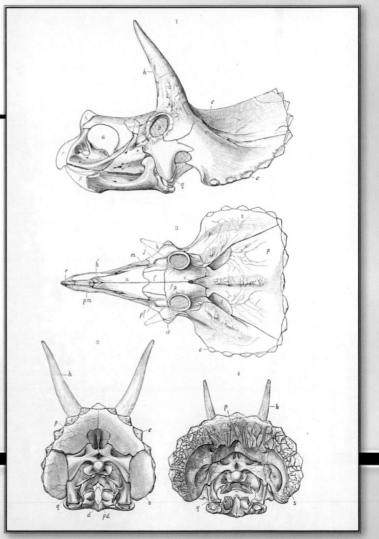

April 1889

Marsh receives Hatcher's skull and publishes the first description of it. He names it *Ceratops horridus* ("standing up horn face"). Marsh thinks the animal had a body like the armored *Stegosaurus*.

Lance Creek, Wyoming: *Triceratops Galore*

Early summer 1889
Paleontologist Charles E. Beecher finds a skull. Marsh later names it *Triceratops serratus* ("serrated"), because the edge of the frill looks like a saw.

July 4, 1889
Hatcher finds another skull very close to Beecher's skull. Marsh later names it *Triceratops prorsus* ("straight forward"), because the nose horn points forward.

1899
Marsh dies. Hatcher and Richard Swann Lull, Marsh's former student, begin to describe the fossils.

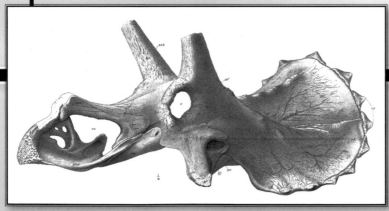

sketch of *Triceratops serratus*

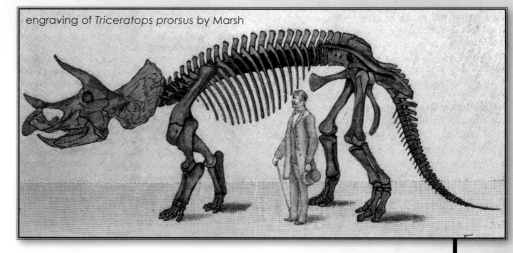

engraving of *Triceratops prorsus* by Marsh

team from the American Museum, including Richard Lull in tall hat in back row and Henry Fairfield Osborn, seated second from right

1891
Marsh names another Hatcher skull *Triceratops elatus* ("elevated"), because the horns stick up. Fossil collector William H. Utterback finds another skull, which Hatcher eventually names *Triceratops brevicornus* ("short horn"). Many others are named in the coming years.

1907
Lull and Hatcher's book, with additional writing by Marsh, is finally published. It describes all known horned dinosaurs.

1904
Hatcher dies while writing a book about horned dinosaurs. Lull agrees to finish the book.

Lightning Creek, Wyoming: *Other Giant Three-Horned Dinosaurs*

Torosaurus

Summer 1891
Hatcher discovers three skulls very similar to *Triceratops*. In one skull the frill is mostly solid, like *Triceratops*. In the other two skulls, the frill is much larger and has big holes in it.

John Bell Hatcher

September 1891
Marsh gives the name *Torosaurus* ("punctured lizard") to the skulls with holes in the frills. However, since the Spanish word for bull is *toro*, the name sounds like it means "bull lizard." It's a good name for a dinosaur with huge horns!

Nedoceratops

1905
Lull names the solid-frilled creature *Diceratops* ("two-horned face"), because the nose horn is very small.

2007
Russian biologist Andrey Sergeevich Ukrainsky notices that the name *Diceratops* actually belongs to an insect named in 1868. The dinosaur needs a new name. He calls it *Nedoceratops* ("not enough horned face"), because the third horn is so small.

Red Deer River and Tolman Bridge, Canada; Bayn Dzak and Ondai Sair Formation, Mongolia: *Cousins Around the World*

Barnum Brown on a dig in Wyoming, 1934

1898

Canadian paleontologist Lawrence Morris Lambe finds part of the frill of a horned dinosaur near the Red Deer River. He thinks it belongs to *Monoclonius*, but he later renames it *Chasmosaurus* ("opening lizard"), because of the holes in its frill. Over the next century, more than a dozen different types of horned dinosaurs are discovered.

Chasmosaurus

1910

American paleontologist Barnum Brown finds the skeleton of a frilled, but not horned, dinosaur near Tolman Bridge. This creature is much smaller than *Triceratops* and its cousins.

Leptoceratops

Osborn's specimen of *Psittacosaurus*

September 2, 1922
The American Museum of Natural History in New York City launches a giant expedition in China and Mongolia. At Bayn Dzak, photographer J. B. Shackelford finds the skeleton of a dinosaur similar to *Leptoceratops*. This creature is later named *Protoceratops* ("first horned face").

Later in 1922
On the same expedition, at Ondai Sair, a driver named Wong finds the skeleton of a smaller dinosaur with a parrotlike beak and no frill. It comes from rocks older than those of all the horned and frilled dinosaurs. Paleontologist Henry Fairfield Osborn later names it *Psittacosaurus* ("parrot lizard"). He doesn't realize that *Psittacosaurus* is an early relative of *Triceratops*.

1914
Brown names his discovery *Leptoceratops* ("small horned face"), even though it doesn't have horns.

Protoceratops

15

Golden, Colorado, and Bowman County, North Dakota: *Triceratops Tracks*

Barnum Brown (left) at the American Museum of Natural History

1905
A skeleton of *Triceratops* is put on display for the first time. It is mounted at the Smithsonian Institution in Washington, D.C. The front legs are put together so that the front feet fall in a straight line in front of the back feet.

Triceratops skeleton, Smithsonian, 1905

1933
A different *Triceratops* skeleton is put on display at the American Museum of Natural History. Osborn and Brown choose a different leg placement. They decide the front legs should stick out to the sides, farther apart than the back feet, like an alligator's arms.

Martin Lockley with bird track fossils

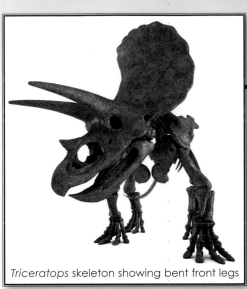
Triceratops skeleton showing bent front legs

1986
At a quarry in Golden, Colorado, dinosaur tracks are exposed. Dinosaur track expert Martin Lockley identifies some as the footprints of *Triceratops*. The footprints show that the front feet were almost directly in line with the back feet, but a little off to the sides. Lockley thinks that the front legs were like those of a rhino.

1993
In North Dakota biologist William Garstka finds one of the most complete *Triceratops* skeletons ever discovered.

2000
Paleontologists Gregory Paul and Per Christiansen show that the front legs of *Triceratops* were bent, and the feet were tilted to the side. This matches the pattern seen in the Golden tracks.

Garstka's *Triceratops*

2009
Paleontologist Shin-ichi Fujiwara describes Garstka's skeleton. He shows that Paul and Christiansen were mostly correct.

Jordan, Montana: *Fighting Triceratops*

Triceratops battling one another

1917
Charles H. Sternberg writes that he thinks the horns of *Triceratops* were there to hold off attacks by *Tyrannosaurus*.

Triceratops and T. rex

1933
Lull writes that he thinks *Triceratops* also used their horns to fight one another.

2005

Paleontologist John Happ studies a partial *Triceratops* skull from Jordan, Montana. He sees that one of the horns was bitten off by a *Tyrannosaurus* but then healed. This shows that *Triceratops* did fight *Tyrannosaurus*.

2009

Paleontologists Andrew Farke, Ewan Wolff, and Darren Tanke study the skulls of dozens of *Triceratops*. They find many facial wounds just where the horns from another *Triceratops* would strike. Sternberg and Lull were both correct in their theories.

Triceratops skull

Lance Creek, Wyoming: *How Many Species?*

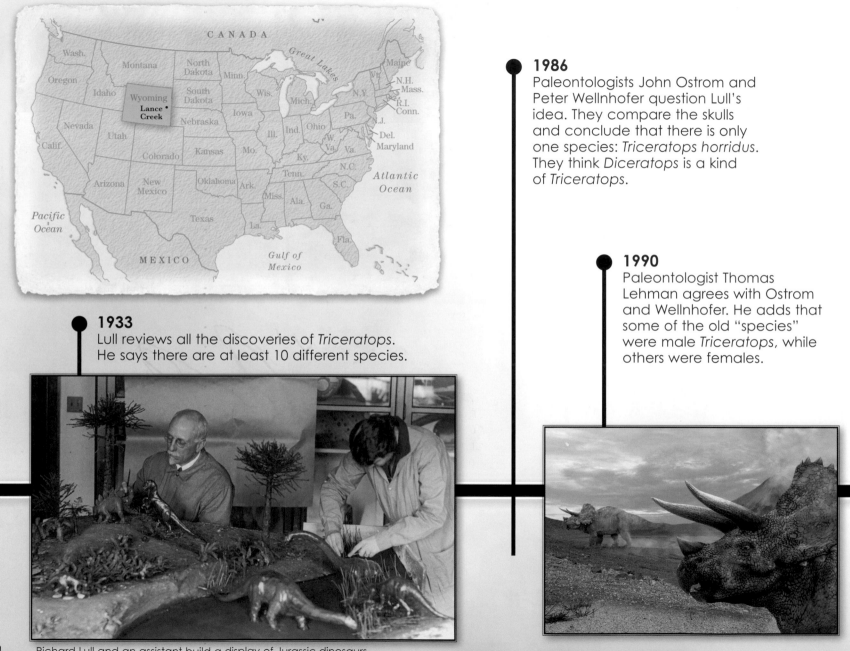

1986
Paleontologists John Ostrom and Peter Wellnhofer question Lull's idea. They compare the skulls and conclude that there is only one species: *Triceratops horridus*. They think *Diceratops* is a kind of *Triceratops*.

1990
Paleontologist Thomas Lehman agrees with Ostrom and Wellnhofer. He adds that some of the old "species" were male *Triceratops*, while others were females.

1933
Lull reviews all the discoveries of *Triceratops*. He says there are at least 10 different species.

Richard Lull and an assistant build a display of Jurassic dinosaurs

Triceratops horridus

Triceratops prorsus

2009
Paleontologists John Scannella and Denver Fowler discover that the two species lived at slightly different times. *Triceratops horridus* lived earlier, and *Triceratops prorsus* lived later.

1996
Paleontologist Cathy Forster measures the same skulls. She comes to a different conclusion. She finds that *Diceratops* is different from *Triceratops*. She claims that there are two species of *Triceratops*: *horridus* and *prorsus*.

EXPERT: *Cathy Forster*

Paleontologist Catherine Forster (born 1956) has made important discoveries about *Triceratops*. She went to college at the University of Minnesota. For her graduate work, she studied with Peter Dodson, an expert on horned dinosaurs at the University of Pennsylvania. Today she teaches at George Washington University in Washington, D.C. She is also president of the Society of Vertebrate Paleontology.

Forster has hunted for fossils in many countries around the world. She and her teams have discovered many types of dinosaurs. However, a lot of her research has been on duckbilled and horned dinosaurs.

While studying *Triceratops*, Forster showed the importance of careful measurements and math. Hundreds of *Triceratops* skulls had been found, and paleontologists did not know if they were all the same species. Forster measured various parts of the skull and used math to compare them. This is how she discovered that there are only two main types of *Triceratops*.

21

Hell Creek and Fort Peck Lake, Montana: *Babies and Grown-Ups?*

Jack Horner

1995
Fossil collector Harley Garbani discovers the smallest *Triceratops* skull ever found.

reconstruction of Garbani's *Triceratops* skull find

1999
Paleontologist Jack Horner begins an 11-year-long digging project near Fort Peck Lake. He wants to find as many fossils as possible. The diggers find fossils of dinosaurs, other animals, and plants. Among them are many *Triceratops* fossils.

2006
Horner and his colleague Mark Goodwin describe growth changes in *Triceratops*, from baby to adult.

2010
Scannella and Horner suggest that *Torosaurus* is not its own kind of dinosaur. Instead, it is a fully grown *Triceratops*.

adult *Triceratops* with their young

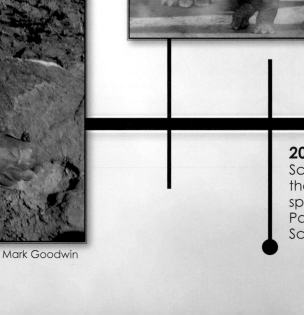

Mark Goodwin

2011
Scannella and Horner further suggest that *Nedoceratops* is also not its own species but a nearly grown *Triceratops*. Paleontologists continue to debate Scannella and Horner's conclusions.

Buffalo, South Dakota; Dry Island Buffalo Jump Provincial Park, Canada; Willow Wash, New Mexico: *Triceratops Cousins or Just More Triceratops?*

Xiao-chun Wu

2001
Glen Guthrie, the camp cook for a paleontological expedition, finds a skeleton of a very large horned dinosaur in Dry Island Buffalo Jump Provincial Park in Alberta, Canada.

1997
A team of fossil hunters from the Black Hills Institute of Geological Research finds the skeleton of a 10-foot- (3-meter-) long horned dinosaur near Buffalo, South Dakota.

2005
Fowler finds part of a horned-dinosaur skull near Willow Wash, New Mexico.

Ojoceratops

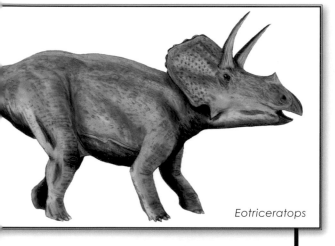

Eotriceratops

2010
Paleontologists Robert Sullivan and Spencer Lucas name the New Mexico dinosaur *Ojoceratops*, after the Ojo Alamo rocks in which it was found. The Dry Island dinosaur is named *Tatankaceratops* ("bison horned face").

2011
Paleontologist Nicholas Longrich argues that *Ojoceratops* and *Tatankaceratops* are actually specimens of *Triceratops*.

2007
Paleontologist Xiao-chun Wu and colleagues study the Dry Island skeleton. They decide that it is an early close relative of *Triceratops*, so they name it *Eotriceratops* ("dawn *Triceratops*"). It is one of the biggest known *Triceratops*-like fossils.

Lusk, Wyoming: *Triceratops Skin*

Later in 2002
Larson notices two important things about Lane. First, the skeleton is one of the most complete *Triceratops* ever found. Second, there is an impression of the dinosaur's scales in the ground around its body. Unlike the scales of other horned dinosaurs, some of the *Triceratops* scales are very big—the size of a coffee saucer.

Triceratops mount at the Houston Museum of Natural Science

2002
Rancher Arlene Zerbst discovers a *Triceratops* on her land. Paleontologist Peter Larson and his team begin to dig up the skeleton. The skeleton is nicknamed "Lane" after Arlene's grandson.

Pete Larson, right, at the Houston Museum of Natural Science

2012
Lane's skeleton is put on display at the Houston Museum of Natural Science.

2013
Lane's skin impressions are put on public display at the Black Hills Institute in South Dakota.

About *Triceratops*

Length: up to 30 feet (9 m); normally 26 feet (8 m) or smaller

Height: up to 10 feet (3 m) at the hips

Weight: 8 tons (7.3 metric tons) or more

Age: lived 67 to 66 million years ago, during the very end of the Cretaceous Period

Location: Western North America

Diet: plants that grow low to the ground

Distinctive features: It has two very long horns over the eyes and a smaller horn over the nose. If *Torosaurus* and *Triceratops* are actually different, *Triceratops* is the only big horned dinosaur with a short, solid frill. (However, if *Torosaurus* is an adult *Triceratops*, then the frill grows very long at the end of its life.)

Enemies: *Tyrannosaurus* is the only known dinosaur that would have been a threat to an adult *Triceratops*. Baby *Triceratops* would have had to watch out for the raptor *Acheroraptor*.

Closest relatives: If *Torosaurus* and *Nedoceratops* are not the same as *Triceratops*, they are its closest relatives. Another close relative is *Eotriceratops*.

Fighting: Several *Triceratops* fossils have cut marks in places where the horns of another *Triceratops* would touch if they locked their heads together. So, like many horned animals today (antelope, deer, chameleons, beetles), *Triceratops* used their horns partly to fight each other.

Glossary

Cretaceous Period—the span of geologic time from 145 to 66 million years ago; the third of three geologic periods from the Mesozoic Era

expedition—a journey with a goal, such as exploring or searching for something

fossil—the remains of a living thing (like bones and teeth) or traces of its action (like footprints) preserved in the rock record; evidence of life from the geologic past

frill—in dinosaurs, a shield of bone covering the neck made from the stretched-out bones of the back of the skull

geologist—a scientist who studies minerals, rocks, and soil

paleontologist—a scientist who studies fossils

quarry—a place where stone or other minerals are dug from the ground

raptor—a bird of prey that hunts and eats small animals

species—a particular kind of living thing

specimen—a particular individual or sample of something; in fossils, a specimen is the remains of one particular example of a species

theory—an idea that explains something that is unknown

vertebra—a back bone; more than one vertebra are vertebrae

Read More

Bakker, Robert T., and Luis V. Rey (illus.). *The Big Golden Book of Dinosaurs*. New York: Golden Book, 2013.

Brusatte, Steve. *Field Guide to Dinosaurs*. New York: Book Sales Inc., 2009.

Holtz Jr., Thomas R. *Dinosaurs: The Most Complete, Up-to-Date Encyclopedia for Dinosaur Lovers of All Ages*. New York: Random House, 2007.

McCurry, Kristen, and Juan Calle (illus.). *How to Draw Incredible Dinosaurs*. North Mankato. Minn.: Capstone Press, 2013.

Internet Sites

Use FactHound to find Internet sites related to this book. All of the sites on FactHound have been researched by our staff.

Here's all you do:

Visit www.facthound.com

Type in this code: 9781491421260

ABOUT THE AUTHOR

Thomas R. Holtz Jr. is a vertebrate paleontologist with the University of Maryland Department of Geology. He has authored dozens of books and articles on dinosaurs for children and adults. He has even appeared in dinosaur-themed comic strips. A graduate of Yale and Johns Hopkins, Dr. Holtz lives in Maryland when he's not traveling the world, hunting fossils.

Index

Bibliography

Carpenter, K. (ed.). 2006. *Horns and Beaks: Ceratopsian and Ornithopod Dinosaurs.* Indiana University Press. 384 pp.

Dodson, P. 1996. *The Horned Dinosaurs.* Princeton University Press. 360 pp.

Dodson, P., C.A. Forster & S.D. Sampson. 2004 Ceratopsidae. Pp. 494-513, in Weishampel, D.B., P. Dodson & H. Osmólska (eds.), *The Dinosauria* (second edition). University of California Press.

Farke, A.A., E.D.S. Wolff & D.H. Tanke. 2009. Evidence of combat in *Triceratops.* PLoS ONE 4 (1): e4252. doi:10.1371/journal.pone.0004252.

Forster, C.A. 1996. Species resolution in *Triceratops*: cladistic and morphometric approaches. *Journal of Vertebrate Paleontology* 16: 259–270. doi:10.1080/02724634.1996.10011313.

Fujiwara, S.-I. 2009. A reevaluation of the manus structure in *Triceratops* (Ceratopsia: Ceratopsidae). *Journal of Vertebrate Paleontology* 29: 1136–1147. doi:10.1671/039.029.0406.

Hatcher, J.B., O.C. Marsh & R.S. Lull. 1907. The Ceratopsia. *U.S. Geological Survey Monograph* 49: 1–300.

Longrich, N.R. & D.J. Field. 2012. *Torosaurus* is not *Triceratops*: ontogeny in chasmosaurine ceratopsids as a case study in dinosaur taxonomy. *PLoS ONE* 7(2): e32623. doi:10.1371/journal.pone.0032623.

Mathews, J.C., S.L. Brusatte, S.A. Williams & D.M. Henderson. 2009. The first *Triceratops* bonebed and its implications for gregarious behavior. *Journal of Vertebrate Paleontology* 29: 286–290. doi:10.1080/02724634.2009.10010382.

Ostrom, J.H. & P. Wellnhofer. 1986. The Munich specimen of *Triceratops* with a revision of the genus. *Zitteliana* 14: 111–158.

Scannella, J.B. & D.W. Fowler. 2014. A stratigraphic survey of *Triceratops* localities in the Hell Creek Formation, northeastern Montana (2006–2010). *Geological Society of America Special Papers* 503: 313–332. doi:10.1130/2014.2503(12).

Scannella, J. & J.R. Horner. 2010. *Torosaurus* Marsh, 1891, is *Triceratops* Marsh, 1889 (Ceratopsidae: Chasmosaurinae): synonymy through ontogeny. *Journal of Vertebrate Paleontology* 30: 1157–1168. doi:10.1080/02724634.2010.483632.